VOLUME 1

The Peak District

A little souvenir

Text by PJ McGowan MBE BEM

CHRIS ANDREWS PUBLICATIONS

The Peak District
Britain's First National Park

Introduction to The Peak District National Park

The Peak District National Park is a truly unique and magical place. Britain's first National Park was created on 17th April 1951 and is the second busiest National Park in the world – an estimated 22 million visitors a year – after Mount Fuji in Japan, with an estimated 105 million day visitors per year.

The Park is wedged nicely at the southern tip of the Pennines at the junction of highland and lowland Britain, between the northwest's two great industrial cites, to the west, Manchester, the birthplace of the Industrial Revolution and to the east, Sheffield, famous for it's high quality steel making and mining. The Park covers an area of 555 square miles (1,438 square kilometres) and half the population of England live within 60 miles of its boundary. The Park is home to about 38,000 people and has been the much needed 'Green Lung' for many years for folk from the large conurbations of the cities of the industrial north which surrounds this special place including Bradford, Leeds, Huddersfield, Matlock, Derby, Ashbourne, Stoke-on-Trent, Macclesfield and Stockport. The Park is a Mecca for walking, rock climbing, cycling, horse riding, caving and fishing.

The contrasting landscape of the National Park has two distinct landforms, The White Peak and the Dark Peak.

Drystone walled open road above Ilam   5

The White Peak forms the central and southern limestone plateau at about 1,000 feet (305 metres) with clear flowing rivers running through the steep craggy beautiful dales, which remain very popular with family groups to discover the joys of the great outdoors. You might well be lucky and spot a kingfisher or a dipper flash by! Miles of drystone walls built in many patterns to form field boundaries cover the whole area with dairy farming the main industry.

The Duke of Devonshire's grand Chatsworth House, the Duke of Rutland's Haddon Hall, Ilam Hall, and the medieval Peveril Castle above Castleton are all great attractions worth a visit if the weather is having a very 'bad-day' across the Pennines!

One of England's finest villages in the Park is Edensor (pronounced Ensor), re-located by the

4th Duke of Devonshire, during his programme to update Chatsworth House.

The main town in the Peak District is Bakewell, famous for its Bakewell Pudding, with a population of about 4,000 people, and the town holds an agricultural market every Monday.

Castleton and the Hope Valley mark the boundary between the White and the Dark Peak. The Dark Peak includes all the high moorlands north of Hayfield, Edale and Hathersage, including the highest points of Kinder Scout 2,088 feet (636 metres), Bleaklow and Black Hill, to Marsden on the Park's northern boundary.

The high ground is a barren plateau of a deep peat blanket covered by fluffy cotton grass and is home to the hardy Gritstone sheep, the Red

Farm buildings at Tissington   7

Ladybower reservoir

10   The Winnats Pass – scene of the ramblers access rallies in the 1930's

Grouse, Golden Plover and the Blue Mountain Hare. The Gritstone Edges of Stanage, Froggatt, Curber, Dowstones Rocks and Laddow Rocks provide some of the finest rock climbing to be had in Britain.

The Mass Trespass on Kinder Scout on 24th April 1932 led to the setting up of National Parks in Britain and the 1st Access Agreement was signed in December 1953 at Edale to allow walkers to wander free over Kinder Scout and later this was extended to all moorland areas. Skilful navigation is required to find your way over much of the high ground.

The Peak National Park has something for everyone, regardless of your age, size, shape or ability, and this little book attempts to show some of its charm.

Hayfield

Earlier generations enjoying The Peak District   11

12 Ashbourne on market day, the village is the southern gateway to the Peak National Park

Ramshaw Rocks near Leek offers some of the finest rock climbing in the Peak Park   13

14   Pony trekking is popular and widespread throughout the Peak District

16   Tissington village, known for its famous well dressing ceremony, believed to date from the 17th century

The 13th century Holy Cross church at Ilam with the Bunster Hill and Thorpe Cloud behind 17

18   The picturesque village of Ilam near the meeting of the Manifold and Dove valleys

Thorpe Cloud sits at the southern tip of the Pennine Range that stretches to the Scottish border 19

20 Spring blossom on the hills above Dovedale

Lush summer vegetation on the banks of the River Dove   21

22   Dovedale, a scenic valley much visited today and noted by Izaak Walton in his *Compleat Angler* 1653–1655

Dovedale and the famous 3 mile long walk between Thorpe Cloud and Milldale   23

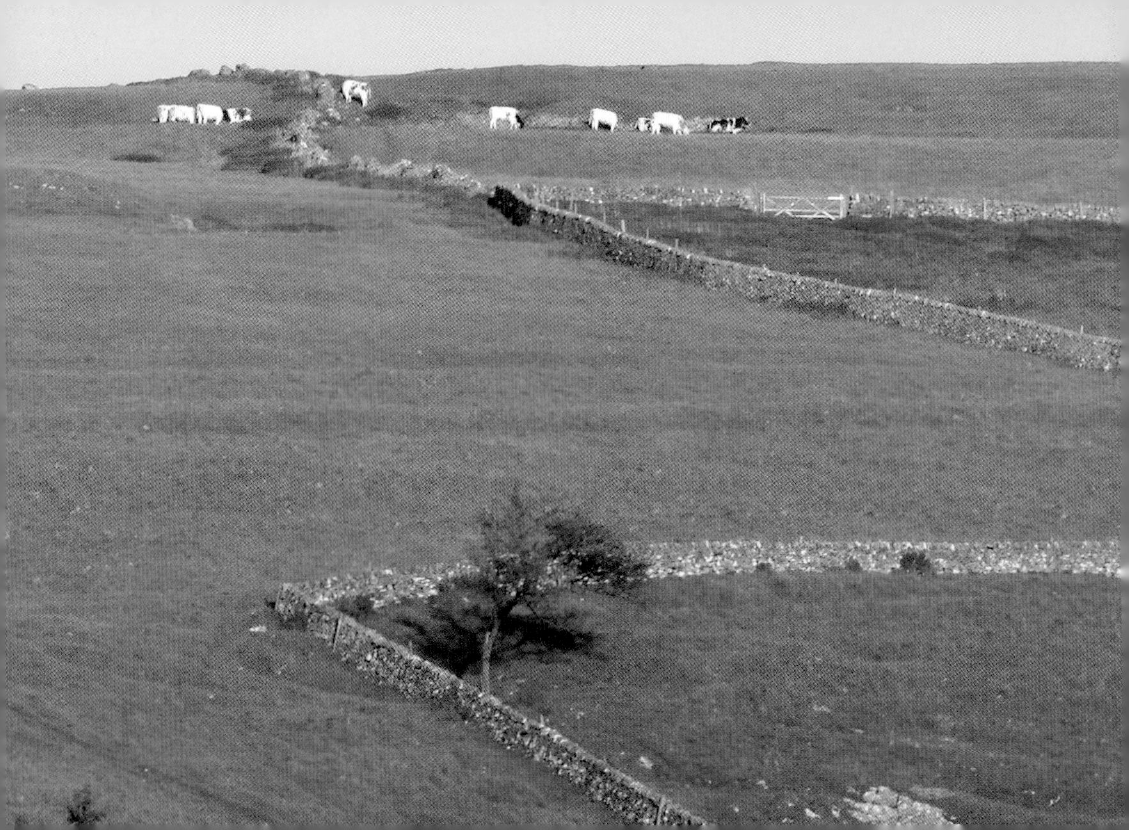

Characteristic stone walls divide fields on the hills above Milldale

26   Peak District dry stone walls enclose many flowers and herb rich meadows

Cattle grazing on the plentiful pastures in the southern Peak District   27

28 The Crescent, completed by the architect John Carr in 1789, and the University at Buxton

Buxton Pavilion Gardens, a Grade II listed park, was designed by Edward Milner in the 1870's   29

30 Tradition is much appreciated and noted in Buxton

The plaque in Bowden Bridge car park at
Hayfield marks the Mass Tresspass of 1932

The Pennine Way traverses over the Kinder Downfall 31

32   Farm buildings and track below Kinder Scout

Dark peaty water typifies the streams of the high moorlands

34 Holmfirth marks the northern boundary of The Peak District and is famous as the setting for *Last of the Summer Wine*

The Dark Peak area towards Durnford Bridge Reservoir   35

36   The 268-mile Pennine Way, Britain's first National Trail, designated in 1965 it starts at Edale

38   Castleton in winter, below the steep Peak Cavern Gorge

A typical winter scene with an old barn amongst dry stone wall patterns in the landscape   39

Castleton is surrounded by hills and marks the boundary between the White Peak and the Dark Peak

42   Early Christmas Celebrations with brass band in Castleton

The paved Pennine Way over the Bleaklow moorland   43

44   B29 Superfortress wreck on Higher Shelf Stones, Bleaklow

Looking towards Edale and the High Peak from the hills above Ladybower Reservoir   45

46   Looking across Ladybower Reservoir from Crookhill Farm towards Bamford Edge

Derwent Reservoir was used to practice for the 'Dam Busters' raid in World War II   47

48   Early morning reflections and the dam at Howden Reservoir

The Reservoirs flooded Birchinlee Village, perhaps some of the shrubs pictured are survivors?   49

50 Hathersage lies below Stanage Edge and made millstones for the surrounding area

The Cheshire Cheese, Hathersage   51

52 Stannage Edge from the north

Stannage Edge at sunset 53

54   View south from Stannage Edge

Mineral rich streams help define The Peak District 55

56 Chatsworth, the bridge over the river Derwent and Chatsworth House from the south

58 Fertile farmland and stone buildings surround the busy market town of Bakewell

The River Wye runs through Bakewell 59

60   Relaxing by the River Wye

Bakewell market trades stock from much of the District, and provides opportunity for local discussion   61

62 Farmland near Parwich in the south of the Park

Arbor Low, a stone age monument near near Moynash dating from around 2000 BC   63

First published 2007 by Chris Andrews Publications 15 Curtis Yard North Hinksey Lane Oxford OX2 0NA
Telephone: +44(0)1865 723404 email: chris.andrews1@btclick.com
ISBN 978–1–905385–38–6 © Chris Andrews Publications.
Text by Peter McGowen MBE BEM. Designed and produced by Chris Andrews and Mike Brain
www.cap-ox.com Images from www.oxfordpicturelibrary.co.uk

Acknowledgments: This publication owes much to the enthusiasm, skill and encouragement of Mike Brain,
who as well as being the designer is an indefatigable companion. Also to Pete McGowan for his knowledge and text and
Mrs Jan Deakin for the historical photo on page 11

Front Cover: Derwent Reservoir   Title: View south from Stannage Edge   Back cover: Farmland at Stanshope